Indian Country Today: Then and Now

Indian Country Today

Copyright © 2025 IndiJ Public Media

All rights reserved

Printed in the United States of America
Book design by Janee' Doxtator
Book cover design by Jacki Foster

The articles in this book first appeared on the news site on ictnews.org and have been edited for style, punctuation, clarity, brevity and accuracy.

IndiJ Public Media is a nonprofit organization based in Arizona. IndiJ Public Media acquired Indian Country Today in 2021 and changed the brand name to ICT later that year.

ISBN: 9798313018294

DEDICATION

For all the dedicated people who have worked for Indian Country Today throughout the years.

ICT at 40: 'We reported like Indians, from the ground up'

By Mark Trahant
ICT
July 9, 2021

Forty years ago The Lakota Times rolled off the press in Pine Ridge, South Dakota, published by Tim Giago. That paper became Indian Country Today in 1992. Later it was the Indian Country Today Media Network, owned by the Oneida Indian Nation. It became a magazine and a daily website. Then in 2017 the publication was shuttered, at least temporarily, and the assets were given to the National Congress of American Indians, better known as NCAI. And by 2018 Indian Country Today was back in business with a tiny crew of three people.

ICT's ownership changed again in March 2021. Indian Country Today (or ICT4 as the news team called it internally) is now independent and owned by IndiJ Public Media, an Arizona not-for-profit corporation, led by Karen Michel, Ho-Chunk.

CHAPTER 1:
THEN

Preface

Welcome to the first book that seeks to preserve the legacy of Indian Country Today. Known as the premier news organization that served Indigenous communities from the 1990s to the early 2020s, Indian Country Today has an enduring impact through IndiJ Public Media, the 501(c)(3) organization that owns the ICT brand.

Many people still refer to ICT as Indian Country Today, although the name was changed to ICT in 2021. All the more reason to publish "Indian Country Today: Then and Now." This Indian Country Today throwback book sheds light on ICT's roots in The Lakota Times newspaper and its transformation to Indian Country Today, as you will see in the "Then" section of stories in Chapter 1.

A historical narrative in the first chapter commemorates the 40th anniversary of Indian Country Today, written by Mark Trahant, former ICT editor and now a contributor. Trahant was instrumental in reviving Indian Country Today after it ceased publication in 2017 and its assets were gifted to the National Congress of American Indians. The "Then" section is a tribute to the founding editor of The Lakota Times and Indian Country Today, Tim Giago, who passed into the spirit world in 2022.

Chapter 2, the "Now" section, shows how Indian Country Today has grown with the changing times through the ICT brand, yet remains true to serving Native communities with news about the Indigenous world. The piece that opens Chapter 2 is a first-person excerpt by then-executive editor Jourdan Bennett-Begaye. In it, she articulates how ICT's readership habits have changed, and how younger readers closely follow entertainment news.

Chapter 3 showcases Indian Country Today's evolution, explains the name change to ICT and defines the role of IndiJ Public Media.

As you read ICT's stories captured in this book, you will see how Indian Country Today's legacy lives on.

Karen Lincoln Michel
President, CEO and Chief Editorial Executive
IndiJ Public Media

TABLE OF CONTENTS

Preface   *i*

Chapter 1: Then

ICT at 40: 'We reported like Indians, from the ground up'   2

'Don't be afraid to stand up,' the legacy of Tim Giago   15

Blink and it's 50 years   23

Chapter 2: Now

The Academy Awards through my eyes   42

Historic Apology: Boarding school history 'a sin on our soul'   49

Chapter 3: ICT and IndiJ Public Media

A new day, a new ICT   56

What's IndiJ Public Media?   59

Our Brand Evolution   62

Our Staff   63

INDIAN COUNTRY TODAY: THEN AND NOW

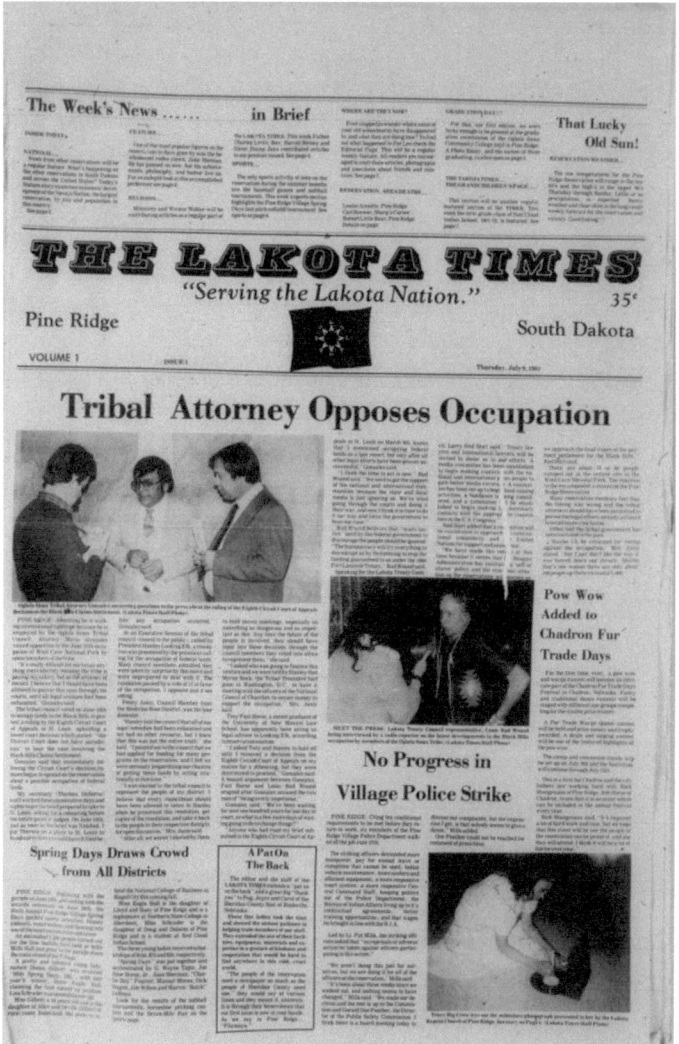

First issue of The Lakota Times printed in Pine Ridge, South Dakota, July 9, 1981. (Photo via Library of Congress)

"While working as a reporter for the Rapid City Journal, I was bothered by the fact that although I had been born and raised on the Pine Ridge Indian Reservation, I was seldom given an opportunity to do news stories about the people of the reservation," wrote Giago in a 2005 article in Nieman Reports. "One editor told me that I would not be able to be objective in my reporting. I replied, 'All of your reporters are white. Are they objective when covering the white community.'"

Giago said by the spring of 1981 he knew he had to start a newspaper at Pine Ridge. The first office was in a former beauty shop. "It seems strange now but when our newspaper hit the stands," he wrote, "we became the only independently owned Indian weekly newspaper in America."

The newspaper company was successful by several metrics. It went on to win hundreds of reporting awards from regional and Native press associations. Giago said investigations from the newspaper "caused banks to be fined and rip-offs of the tribal government to be halted … The Lakota Times proved that freedom of the press could not only succeed in Indian Country but that it can make a major difference in the way news is covered on the Indian reservations of America."

Over the years The Lakota Times expanded its reach. "Even though we eventually had news coverage from all nine Indian reservations in South Dakota, we always considered them to be one community. All of us grew up in the same fashion, which meant we lived in poverty and shared many of the same difficulties," he said.

Then in 1992, "to reflect its national circulation," The Lakota Times became Indian Country Today. The national map was expanded with bureaus in Washington, D.C., Spokane and Albuquerque, as well as financial support from the Gannett Foundation (now the Freedom Forum) and The New York Times.

INDIAN COUNTRY TODAY: THEN AND NOW

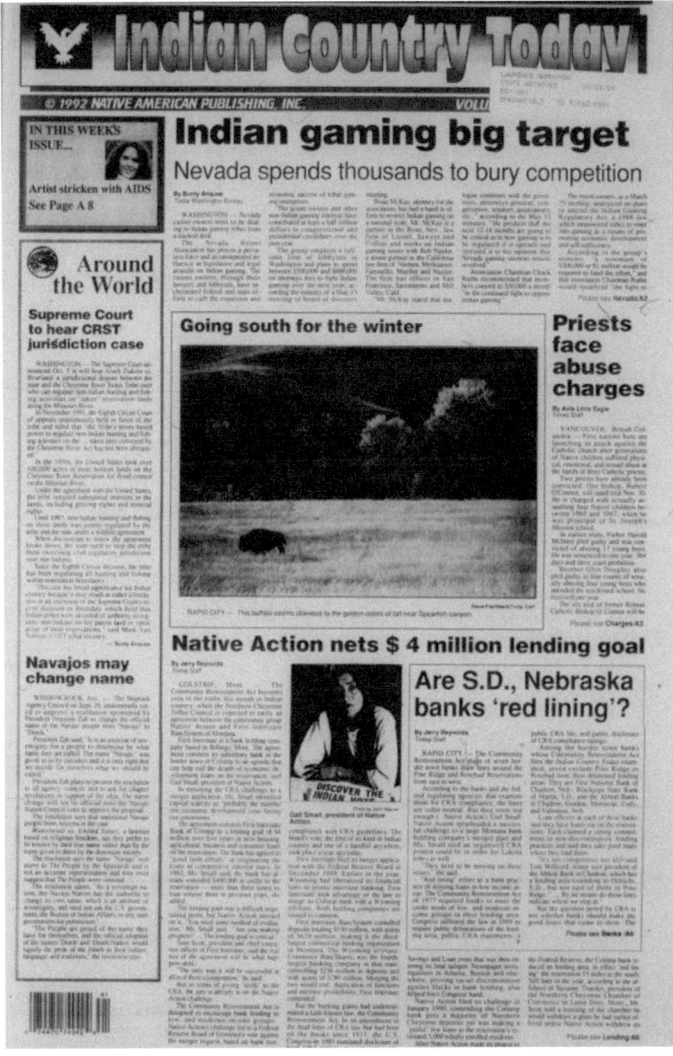

First issue of Indian Country Today printed in Pine Ridge, South Dakota, March 2, 1992. (Photo via Library of Congress)

The paper's offices moved to Rapid City in 1989 and by 1999 the circulation was reported as reaching 50,000 copies with a pass-along readership that topped six figures.

Three themes emerged in the early years of The Lakota Times and Indian Country Today: An honest accounting of the boarding school experience (so relevant now); an exploration of the mascot issue and its impact on Native people; and a strident challenge to the work of the American Indian Movement.

And like any publication, Indian Country Today earned both praise and criticism for its writing.

Giago had a longtime feud with Chuck Trimble, Oglala Lakota. Trimble had been an editor in Denver and was executive director of the American Indian Press Association (before he moved on to NCAI). Both men attended Holy Rosary Mission School and for many years Giago (and a lot of us) thought Trimble was the secret author of a newsletter, Lakota TIM (or Truth In Media).

Giago complained that Trimble wrote a column about him that was "a mixture of lies and half-truths disguised as fact. It is too bad that a man with such a good record as executive director of NCAI should sink so low as to air his vicious, personal attacks upon someone he has known all of his life."

Trimble in 2012 revealed that he edited Lakota TIM but its author was mostly a politician, Shirley Plume, Oglala Lakota. "Her new single-page journal ... would be authored by Lakota persons under the nom de plume of 'Iktomi.' Like its legendary namesake, Iktomi used satire with humor and self-deprecation in their rollicking crusade," Trimble wrote. "Lakota TIM* had a limited press run which was mailed to only several members of the then-Native American Press Association (NAPA); but it usually got a much wider circulation via fax from there on. Sending it to his peers, it was hoped, would put pressure on Giago himself to be more fair and truthful."

What's missing from that narrative is that Shirley Plume is also Chuck's sister.

The feud ended by the time of Trimble's death in March 2020. Giago wrote that Trimble's "passing has left a big hole in the field of Native American journalism."

> *"I made a mistake, I think, in selling it. So I decided to start another one."*
>
> – Tim Giago

The impact of ICT founder Giago is remarkable. And many other publications have significant ties to Giago and the original ICT. Giago's ventures include Native Sun News, as well as the Lakota Journal, and the Lakota Times (which had been Lakota Country Times until a couple of years ago).

Avis Little Eagle, who worked with Giago at Lakota Times, later edited the Teton Times in McLaughlin, South Dakota. While at Lakota Times, Little Eagle wrote a 10-part series on fake medicine men. She also suggested the name, "Indian Country Today."

Indeed Giago has retired several times. When he sold Indian Country Today to the Oneida Indian Nation and its company, Standing Stone Media, Inc., Giago cited retirement as a goal. But soon after he started another newspaper at Pine Ridge.

"I made a mistake, I think, in selling it," Giago told American Journalism Review. He was 65 years old. "So I decided to start another one."

Then 10 years ago, Giago announced his retirement from Native Sun News. "I may retire from the news business,"

Giago wrote in a column, "but certainly not from life."

He credited his mentor, Rupert Costo, Cahuilla, the legendary editor of the national publication, Wassaja, based in San Francisco. "Rupert could be a hard man with strong opinions, but he was a man who had the courage of his convictions and he pounded that sense of standing up for the rights of others into my head."

Giago again reached for the gold watch at 87 years old. He wrote in June that he was going to retire from the business in July. "For more than 40 years I have worn the visor and the arm garters of an editor and publisher. I am proud of the many newspapers I have published all of those years, but it is time for a new generation of Native journalists and editors to take over," he wrote.

One legacy, which literally means a gift to the next generation, was the 1990 Year of Reconciliation led by Giago and South Dakota Gov. George Mickleson. Mickelson proclaimed 1990 as the "Year of Reconciliation," leading to the proclamation for a "Century of Reconciliation." And, at Giago's request, Mickelson and the South Dakota Legislature established Native American Day in October. It was the only state to celebrate it rather than Columbus Day.

Indian Country Today was sold to the Oneida Indian Nation and its company, Standing Stone Media, Inc., in 1998. That venture included a magazine, "This Week in Indian Country," an active website, and the framework for a broader news network, Indian Country Today Media Network, or ICTMN. The venture also lost a lot of money.

As Mary Annette Pember, Red Cliff Band of Wisconsin Ojibwe, wrote in Columbia Journalism Review: "From the beginning, the news organization was mostly a losing financial proposition for the Oneida Nation — part vanity project, part desire to influence movers and shakers in Washington.

However, while I've never spoken with Halbritter or leaders of the Oneida Nation, I think ICTMN was also a genuine source of ethnic pride for them. Rather than being misquoted and overlooked by the media, Indians were finally part of setting the news agenda."

There was a lot of remarkable journalism that took place during Oneida's ownership. Tim Johnson and Jose Barreiro teamed up to broaden the scope of coverage, expanding the Indigenous world beyond U.S. borders. The paper staffed and covered the United Nations including the development of the United Nations Declaration on the Rights of Indigenous Peoples.

Indian Country Today's print magazine started and ended publication a couple of times (magazines are expensive), but starting in 2013 the publication was largely online. At one point ICTMN had a New York City office and a team that was meant to establish the publication as a player in national media.

ICT produced a "best of" book in 2005, "America is Indian Country," repurposing some of the writings, photography and cartoon.

Three current employees of ICT worked for the Oneida venture: Vincent Schilling, Akwesasne Mohawk, and associate editor; Heather Donovan, ICT's advertising director; and Pember, national correspondent.

> *"We reported like Indians, from the ground up."*
>
> – Mary Annette Pember

"We reported like Indians, from the ground up," Pember wrote. "We spoke to the aunties, cousins, grandparents and kids who do the business of living in Indian communities. Jacqui Banaszynski, former Knight Chair in editing at the

Missouri School of Journalism and fellow at the Poynter Institute, once described great journalists as wing walkers, those air-show barnstormers who wandered the edges of airplanes mid-flight. ICTMN editors urged us to walk way the hell out."

Perhaps the most important legacy was the ICTMN coverage of Standing Rock. As Pember wrote: "ICTMN supported Jenni Monet of the Pueblo of Laguna as she reported tirelessly from the Water Protector camps near Standing Rock, and received the Paul Tobenkin Memorial Award for her coverage."

Another cool thing from the Standing Stone Media era was the American Indian Visionary Awards.

In 2006, for example, the paper gave that award to Hank Adams, "the lifelong activist who negotiated peaceful ends to some of the most dangerous standoffs in modern Indian history, is the 2006 recipient of Indian Country Today's American Indian Visionary Award."

Other award winners were Billy Frank, Jr., in 2004 and Vine Deloria, Jr., in 2005.

This award represented a window into the brilliance of Indigenous leaders. (So easy to do when you think of the chiefs of the 19th century, but the 20th century experience was just as rich.)

As the award announcement read: "Adams was a crucial behind-the-scenes figure in practically every scene of the militant Indian revival of the last four decades. He is best known in the history books for his negotiations with the White House to resolve the takeover of the BIA building in Washington in 1972 during the Trail of Broken Treaties protest and to wind down the 10-week siege of Wounded Knee in 1973. Both incidents could have caused untold casualties, but his ability to gain the confidence of both sides is credited with keeping bloodshed to a minimum."

Giago said he regretted selling Indian Country Today and claimed that the publication avoided its critics. "In the 13 years Ray Halbritter has owned Indian Country Today, the newspaper has never published a letter, a column or a news report that was critical of him, the Nation, or the newspaper. And that my friend, is known in the newspaper business as censorship," Giago wrote in a January 2011 column. "How do I know this? As the former editor I began to receive letters shortly after I sold it, letters and emails that continue to come to me even today from Native Americans who were angry that letters and columns they wrote to ICT critical of Halbritter and of the newspaper, were never published."

Pember wrote about what it meant to her to be a reporter at ICT during this era.

"Indian Country is a tough and complex beat. Meaningful coverage demands a depth of historical, legal and social knowledge that reporters are seldom allowed the time necessary to acquire. ICTMN gave reporters that time," Pember wrote. "At ICTMN, writers reported on scientific findings regarding the connection between trauma and ongoing social ills in Indian Country. Rather than excuse the widespread 'dis-ease' that touches Indian Country, the reporting helped communities gain a measure of authority and knowledge over seemingly intractable problems. ICTMN produced a special report based on my research and writing about this issue.

"We blew the lid off Hollywood-style stereotypes that would have the world believe we are stoic, humorless creatures who somehow remain unengaged in contemporary life. ICTMN covered Indian rappers, artists, filmmakers, entrepreneurs and chefs."

ICT's nonprofit business model

I have written a lot about the NCAI and IndiJ Public Media ownership of ICT. So, I won't go there today.

ICT4 has grown significantly over the past four years and yet we have so much more to do. Our goal is to raise about $4 million a year so that we can operate bureaus in key regions, continue to improve our digital reports and our daily broadcast.

But I want to mention another legacy — one that will lead us forward along our other path, broadcasting.

Even though our roots come from The Lakota Times and Tim Giago, there are other contributions and influencers. All of the people my age benefited from the work and guidance of Richard LaCourse, Yakama, Howard Rock, Inupiat, and many other legends. I still greatly appreciate my friendship with Suzan Harjo, Cheyenne and Hodulgee Muscogee. Every phone call is a history lesson where we swap stories about those who've helped us and share our love for our people.

Harjo has been a columnist for ICT in every era. Most recently she has written lengthy pieces that defy expectations — I say that because a June 2018 "column" about the Reclaiming Native Truth report was more than 8,000 words.

Most of our readers — four out of five people — read ICT on a mobile device. That's a really long story to be scrolling on your iPhone.

But Harjo's piece was the best read story of that week. And that month. And one of the top stories of the year. All told, more than 100,000 people read Harjo's essay on their cell phones, or on Facebook (and even most of them were on cell phones) or linking from other web pages.

INDIAN COUNTRY TODAY: THEN AND NOW

"If you don't know sovereignty, you don't know history."

– Suzan Harjo

Readers spent eight minutes and 12 seconds reading "If you don't know sovereignty, you don't know history."

I also think it's worth noting another anniversary. In 2023, we can mark the 50th anniversary of Indian Country Today with Harriet Skye, Standing Rock. This TV show was broadcast in North Dakota and is an example of how you change the story.

As Jodi Rave wrote for Buffalo's Fire: "Skye started hosting 'Indian Country Today' in 1973. For more than a decade, she filmed some 250 episodes, most of which were recorded on 2-inch, reel-to-reel videotape. Producers used the same tape for each show, so only a few of the final episodes survived to be archived at the North Dakota State Historical Society."

Skye "made it seem natural for an Indian woman to report and broadcast the news," Rave wrote after her death in 2018. "I can't think of a single Native person on TV today who hosts a talk show about contemporary Native news."

I love the phrase "a spacious channel" first used by Cherokee journalist Elias Boudinot in 1827. And expanding that spacious channel remains our goal.

Karen Lincoln Michel is IndiJ Public Media's chief executive officer and president and has the last word here.

"I would say ICT definitely has come a long way in 40 years," Michel said on the Friday newscast. "So, we've really covered a lot of ground over the decades. There are many people along the way who have contributed ... I'd say we have a really strong reputation as a premier news source covering Native communities. And we do things, cover stories that the mainstream media does not, and those stories are written and produced by Indigenous journalists for an Indigenous audience. And so I think that's really why we matter."

'Don't be afraid to stand up,' the legacy of Tim Giago

By Jourdan Bennett-Begaye and Mary Annette Pember
ICT
July 24, 2022

Tim Giago showed no signs of ailment as editor emeritus in May 2022 at his Native Sun News Today office in Rapid City, South Dakota. Giago died Sunday morning, nearly two weeks after his 88th birthday.

Tim Giago, editor of Native Sun News Today in his Rapid City office, May 2022. (Photo by Mary Annette Pember, ICT)

At age 87, the longtime journalist was in his element in the busy newsroom, fielding questions from his reporters, while ICT's national correspondent Mary Annette Pember interviewed him about his time as a student at Holy Rosary Indian boarding school (now named Red Cloud School) on the Oglala Lakota nation in South Dakota.

Irascible and sharp as a tack, he was quick to criticize the current mainstream coverage of Indian boarding schools.

"Reporters need to speak directly with survivors who attended these schools rather than relying on secondhand information," he told ICT.

Giago described digging a grave for his childhood friend Bozo Richards who died at age 16 from an ear infection at Holy Rosary.

He also shared memories of how his little sister was raped by a school janitor and the scores of his classmates who died from alcohol and drug addiction that he believes was exacerbated by traumatic experiences at the school.

Long before the topic surfaced in the national media, Giago was writing about his experiences at Holy Rosary in a 2006 book, "Children Left Behind: The Dark Legacy of Indian Mission Boarding Schools."

Giago took a lot of heat over the book both from Catholic leaders as well as his own people, but in typical fashion he stuck to his guns, refusing to sugarcoat or walk back any of his reporting.

According to Giago, when reporters called the school to verify his past attendance, school leaders claimed he never attended.

Prior to ICT's visit with him in Rapid City, however, Pember just spent time in the Catholic Indian boarding school archives kept at Marquette University in Milwaukee. She told him she'd found documentation there of his years at Holy Rosary. He was nonplussed.

"Hey I knew I went there despite their claims to the contrary," he said.

Politely but firmly he let Pember know their interview was over, he had a newspaper to put out. Before leaving, he signed Pember's copy of his boarding school book in typical forward thinking language. "The book you are about to write is needed. Let's continue to educate, thanks, Tim Giago."

Giago died July 24, 2022, in Rapid City, South Dakota, at the age of 88. He was born on July 12, 1934. His Oglala Lakota name was Nanwica Kcjii which translates to He Stands up for Them, or The Defender. Doris Giago, his former wife, said he had cancer and complications related to diabetes. His wife Jackie Giago didn't want to talk.

"While working as a reporter for the Rapid City Journal, I was bothered by the fact that although I had been born and raised on the Pine Ridge Indian Reservation, I was seldom given an opportunity to do news stories about the people of the reservation," Giago, the 1991 Nieman Fellow, wrote in a 2005 article in Nieman Reports. "One editor told me that I would not be able to be objective in my reporting. I replied, 'All of your reporters are white. Are they objective when covering the white community.'"

> *"It seems strange now but when our newspaper hit the stands. We became the only independently owned Indian weekly newspaper in America."*
>
> – Tim Giago

Giago said by the spring of 1981 he knew he had to start a newspaper at Pine Ridge. The first office was in a former beauty shop. "It seems strange now but when our newspaper hit the stands," he wrote, "we became the only independently owned Indian weekly newspaper in America."

Doris Giago remembers the first day in The Lakota Times newsroom in Pine Ridge.

"Well, none of us knew what we were doing. So we all learned by the seat of our pants," said Doris Giago, his ex-wife and co-founder in starting the newspaper in 1981. "We had to start everything from scratch."

Advertising, circulation, and distribution. They didn't know any of it but did the best they could.

They had their relatives, and nieces and nephews who were just 10 or 12 years old grabbing bundles off the press and selling the papers at the tribal offices.

The newspaper company was successful by several metrics. It went on to win hundreds of reporting awards from regional and Native press associations. And Giago said investigations from the newspaper "caused banks to be fined and rip-offs of the tribal government to be halted … The Lakota Times proved that freedom of the press could not only succeed in Indian Country but that it can make a major difference in the way news is covered on the Indian reservations of America."

In 1990 Giago wrote a challenge to the governor, calling for South Dakota to have a "Year of Reconciliation." Gov. George S. Mickelson responded: "I couldn't agree with you more, Tim. We must reconcile those differences. As the state of South Dakota celebrates the beginning of its second century, we must also remember that statehood was a very sad time for the Native Americans." As a gesture, the state dropped Columbus Day and changed it to Native American Day, the first state to do so.

The big lesson Amanda Takes War Bonnett learned from Giago: "Don't be afraid to use your voice. Don't be afraid to

INDIAN COUNTRY TODAY: THEN AND NOW

stand up for when you see disparities in Indian Country."

"He really wasn't scared," said Takes War Bonnett with a laugh who worked with Giago for nearly 14 years. "He wasn't scared to do things. He wasn't scared to speak up."

That got him into trouble, she said. "Some people didn't like him because he would speak up against people, against corruption or things and he had that kind of voice, but I know he had enemies. You know, some people didn't like what he did."

Take the early days of The Lakota Times for example.

"One of the things that was going on when we first starting, we were just coming out of all the problems of 1973 with the occupation of Wounded Knee," Giago told ICT in July 2021. He had a different perspective on it. "I thought a lot of the things that the American Indian Movement did were more harmful than helpful."

Tim Giago in the Native Sun News Today office in Rapid City, South Dakota, July 2021. (Photo by Shirley Sneve, ICT)

He said it even affected his business. His landlord called him at three in the morning. "He said, 'you better get down here.' He said, 'you don't have any windows left.' So I got down here to three in the morning and sure enough, all the windows were gone. And so I moved the paper across the street into a, I thought it would be a more secure office."

"And on December of that year, I got firebombed. People came by and threw molotov cocktails in front of my building. And luckily, a BIA officer was driving by and saw it, and he jumped up and kicked him away from the doors. So those are some of the hard things that came out of work. One night [I] got in my pickup and somebody put a bullet through my windshield and just missed my head," Giago said. "So, I mean, if that's what it took to get the freedom of the press going on the reservation, I guess that's what it took."

In 1983, Giago organized more than two dozen Indigenous journalists and formed the Native American Press Association. That later became the Native American Journalists Association, better known as NAJA. Giago was elected the first president.

"The impact Tim had on Indigenous journalism as one of NAJA's founders is immeasurable. He has been a champion of free press in Indigenous communities his entire career and faced challenges, threats and political pressure, but always pushed to bring essential news and information to the people. He's irreplaceable," said Rebecca Landsberry-Baker, the organization's executive director and Muscogee (Creek), in an email. "I know generations of Indigenous journalists will look to his dogged dedication to the truth for decades to come and be inspired by his tremendous legacy."

Part of Giago's legacy and push to make voices heard is his knack for creating newspapers.

"Tim Giago was a serial creator — first a TV show. Then The Lakota Times. Then the Native American Press Association, later the Native American Journalists He always pushed for more, reaching for an even better way to serve Indian people with news. So after The Lakota Times it was Indian Country Today. Then Lakota Journal. Then Native Sun News. He never lost his vision about how important it is for a community to have a journalistic recording of itself," said Mark Trahant, ICT editor-at-large.

> *"Along the way he lured dozens of Native people into this mission of journalism. He let so many Native young people know how important information can be."*
>
> – Mark Trahant

"Along the way he lured dozens of Native people into this mission of journalism. He let so many Native young people know how important information can be — and why they had as much right to it as anyone."

Takes War Bonnett is an example of seeing and fostering talent.

In 2004 he encouraged her to create a newspaper for Pine Ridge, the Lakota Country Times. Now called the Lakota Times.

Pulitzer Prize finalist and cartoonist Marty Two Bulls Sr. started his career with Giago in 1988. Two Bulls and his wife were both hired — his wife in the business department and Two Bulls in production assembling ads.

"And one day I did an editorial and I took it to him. I said, 'see if you can do a cartoon to this' because he had a good hand in art. So he did a cartoon for the editorial," Giago told ICT. "And from then on every week, I'd give him my editorial and he'd do the cartoons for it."

His ex-wife and friend, Lynn Rapp, said Giago loved the cartoons in the paper. "He felt that it was really critical to make fun of the situation but also make fun of ourselves."

Perhaps that was an extension of his humor. "He had a

marvelous sense of humor, and could make jokes out of many things," she said. "He could make you laugh like crazy."

Besides his humor, Rapp mentioned that she wants people to know that Giago "was very compassionate for people who were in trouble. He was always kind to those who needed kindness."

That compassion and his strong-willed personality drove his life mission of telling the truth for Native peoples. Because they deserved to know.

Giago paved the way for Native journalism; the best way to memorialize him is to continue the work.

Blink and it's 50 years

By Mark Trahant
ICT
August 13, 2024

My love for journalism is as old as I can remember. I drew a crayon newspaper when I was about 8 years old, "The Sun." And as a teenager I remember buying a copy of each of the newspapers in the stands, plugging dimes in a machine so I could skim through what was the same and what was different in each edition. In high school we started an "alternative paper" in class, "The Press Gang," and I later discovered the power of a press pass, using the school's Chronicle as an entry ticket into concerts and other venues.

When I was 17 years old I talked a radio station into doing a broadcast of the March basketball tournament at Fort Hall. I had listened to play by play from radio announcers, sometimes holding a transistor radio to my ear, as they described basketball, baseball and football games. I mimicked what they did. Describing the play and coming up with a few exaggerations.

And I had an audience. I was calling a game with a team from Ethete, Wyoming, and I said the players were Shoshone. About 15 minutes later someone handed me a note. A listener had called the station, "they were Arapahoes, not Shoshones." Correction made.

> *"I was hired ... and the Sho-Ban News began a new era."*
>
> – Mark Trahant

I had so much fun I took my radio broadcasts on the road. I called a game in Yakima, Washington, for their tournament. (I have no idea how I talked my way into that one.)

A year or so later I was working at the radio station. This time I had a paid gig, $75 a month to produce and host "The Sho-Ban Radio Hour." We played music. Promoted local events and reported the news.

I was hooked. The news was it.

A couple of years later I was attending Idaho State University and there was an ad posted for an editor for the Shoshone-Bannock Tribes' newspaper. The publication had been dormant for a few years after the last editor, Lorraine Edmo, moved away to work at a TV station. The funding for the position was the Comprehensive Training and Employment Act — CETA — a training program. I was hired, and the Sho-Ban News began a new era.

The first issue was published on Dec. 10, 1976. From my high school journalism class, I recalled how to count headlines (an old technique for writing a headline that fits the space) and lay out a page. I did everything exactly by the book. On the front page was a picture of our office building, a modern brick teepee. The photo caption read: "The Dawn over the Human Resource Center Symbolizing (sic) the Dawn of The Sho-Ban

News."

Awful. I was proud, my byline even read: "BY MARK N. TRAHANT, Editor-in-Chief." Too many Superman comics! I was completely in charge of a staff of one.

The content was routine: An update of tribal council resolutions, education reports, facts you should know about dental health, and, of course, sports. Important notes for any community, the standings of winter basketball, and the winners of the Buckskin Gloves Boxing Tournament. Only a newspaper is connected to the refrigerator — clips posted for the family as high honor.

From the beginning of our journey, we wanted to clearly chronicle national trends affecting Indian affairs and government policy. When Vice President-Elect Walter Mondale toured Idaho, for example, we thought we ought to tag along and see if we could get the soon-to-be vice president to talk about the new policies. So Wes Edmo and I traveled to Lewiston, Idaho, on Jan. 10, 1977.

Mondale was set to arrive the next day but we had to get our badges for the press events. At the credentials office — an old hotel in downtown Lewiston — I noticed that all the other reporters dressed in suits and ties. In those days, my wardrobe consisted of jeans, T-shirts and cowboy boots or sneakers. I wanted to blend-in; I wanted a chance to ask Mondale a question at the news conference and felt that if I looked as "professional" as the other reporters (and if I shouted loud enough) I could ask the vice president a question about the new administration's proposed western water policy.

My solution was to buy a gray raincoat at J.C. Penney's for about $30. I figured no one would know what was underneath. The only problem was that the following day, when Mondale arrived, it was a warm, sunny January day with temperatures soaring into the 60s. It was very hot underneath that coat. But it was my armor.

The news conference was held in a secluded area at the Lewiston Airport. It was my first encounter with the national press and I was struck by how rude most of the reporters seemed. Even though I had been standing in a spot close to the podium, when they came in (off the press airplane) there was no room for local media. They shoved and pushed until I found myself at the back of the room. When the vice president arrived, it was difficult to ask questions. Most shouted and somehow a press secretary shifted through the noise to recognize one of the reporters. I am not particularly loud and shouting is not one of my better skills; still on every question I tried to be just a little bit louder than my previous attempt. Near the end of the news conference, I was recognized. "Mr. Vice President, will Indian water rights be protected under the Carter Administration's new federal water policy?" Walter Mondale looked for a moment, then he turned to Interior Secretary-Designate Cecil Andrus and said, "I think I had better let the secretary answer that one."

So much for my one-rain-coat question. For the record, Andrus answered by saying that Indian water rights are independent rights; not part of the federal claim. It was a good quote and one that found its way into the next edition of the News.

The Sho-Ban News started as a bi-monthly newspaper. The definition of "bi-monthly" was that anytime I got everything together twice in one month, there would be two editions. Actually, the publication cycle averaged one issue every three weeks. But that troubled me: The other communities in Southern Idaho, no matter how small, were served by weekly newspapers. Was Fort Hall and its 3,000 people any less deserving? Of course not. Just by asking the question, I knew I had to press The Sho-Ban News' deadline. In September 1977 the paper became a weekly.

The News grew so fast that we went through four office suites in less than a year. When the newspaper started it was one desk and one telephone in the middle of a tribal education office in the new human resource center. A couple of months later, we (I now had a colleague) moved to a larger one-room office next door to the tribal council's chambers. As we geared up to go weekly, we moved into a temporary suite of offices (our computer and photographic equipment was expanding too) and, finally, the News returned to the suite where it had begun. The only difference was the entire wing of that building was now the Sho-Ban News, housing its five to eight employees (we hired students in the summer with money from another federal program), darkroom and computer typesetting terminals.

When I first got the job at the News, I thought it would be easy to continue my schooling at the university. I found out that was impossible because I had no time for classwork. It is impossible to work a mere 40 hours a week at a small newspaper, so I dropped out of college. But, I would also like to think, this is when my real education began. I entered fast-paced courses in tribal government, law, journalism and culture.

One of those lessons came courtesy of the Bureau of Indian Affairs, or BIA, (really!). The agency sponsored and paid for a conference in February 1977 in Spokane, Washington, about the importance of tribal journalism. I met other editor leaders; folks like Loren Tapahe, Navajo Nation, and Richard LaCourse, Yakama Nation. LaCourse opened my eyes about the history of the Native press and its role as a vehicle for Indian intelligence.

It's funny now, but one of the speakers — a non-Native reporter, again, paid for by the government — was there to tell us we should be "house organs." Only printing the tribal side of the story.

LaCourse was offended. He said: "I'll have to admit that you are making me extremely angry with your presumption about Indian newspapers are 'house organs.' Are you aware of the 1968 law which guarantees freedom of the press in Indian Country?"

Someone else added, "If the tribal council came to us and said you are going to print it this way, we would walk out."

That was my first lesson on editorial independence. Courtesy the good ol' BIA.

One reason why this lesson was so important was the era. The 1970s was the time of the "backlash" or "whitelash." It was a movement of people who lived near tribal nations who decided it was time for a new Indian war. The groups involved covered themselves with noble names: South Dakotans for Civil Liberties; Montanans Opposed to Discrimination and the Interstate Congress for Equal Rights and Responsibilities, better known as ICERR. These groups defined American Indians as "special citizens" who, because of treaty rights, were getting a better deal than the rest of the nation. A book, "Indian Treaties: America's Nightmare," was sent by the group to members of Congress, the secretary of Interior and other Washington officials. "The liberal treatment of minorities has reached unheard of proportions in denying equal rights to all citizens of our so-called democracy," a brochure for the book said. "Sportsmens (sic) – organizations – fishermen – hunters – land owners – commercial fishermen and just plain tax paying citizens who have just about had it with Indian take-overs make up the membership of ICERR."

The root cause was anger about perceived slights.

The Sho-Ban News staff members covered the backlash as best we could. We tried to keep track of the legislation in Congress, including those that proposed abrogating treaties. The backlash is a cyclical attempt to reverse the Constitution.

INDIAN COUNTRY TODAY: THEN AND NOW

It comes around every 20 years or so; the backlash of the 1970s, termination of the 1950s and the assimilation movement of the 1920s.

But the roots are deeper. The notions are the same as those expressed by Georgians who wanted the Cherokees removed. I suspect these movements reoccur because there is a segment of our society that will always challenge the constitutional rights of "treaty Americans."

But the problem for journalism is that by covering the "backlash" as a force, there is a misperception about journalists being "advocates." Yet none of our counterparts has to explain why a city exists, or a state, yet tribal editors must defend tribal government to other journalists, readers and critics. This is not advocacy journalism — at least not to me. It's explanation.

Several weeks after the Spokane journalism conference there was a new push for the tribal news media to share its stories and start a news service. LaCourse wrote a memorandum on March 25, 1977, that he sent to all Northwest Indian media ventures outlining his idea for a service based on the American Indian Press Association model. "These matters may be pondered, ignored, discussed or rejected, as you will," LaCourse wrote.

I took this to heart and tried to fashion some sort of news service. It started with an old technology, a Telex machine. I purchased one of these devices for $100 and tried to convince every other tribal newspaper to buy one. The goal was to produce shared news copy in real time. It might have worked, except no other tribal newspaper purchased a machine. So we were talking to no one else. (We could send telegrams but that was costly.)

The technology of news has changed a lot in 50 years. When we first started printing The Sho-Ban News, our host was converting from "lead" type to "cold" type. For us that meant a huge machine — the Compugraphic 7200. We'd type the story and then someone else would retype it into a machine and produce a version that could be pasted on a board with wax. A few years later, one Mac did the same thing — and was a lot less expensive. I remember traveling to meetings with a tiny typewriter, then later a Radio Shack TRS 80 (writing four lines at a time) that would connect to a phone to send the story home. The rise of the Internet and web publishing made ICT possible. We never could have done a daily that served all of Indian Country without that technology.

After the 1978 election, Idaho's governor, Cecil D. Andrus, was picked by President Jimmy Carter to be the Interior Secretary. It's always interesting when someone from your home state is selected because you know people in the secretary's office. I interviewed Andrus in Boise in January 1979. We published a complete text of the interview as a four-page special section. Andrus also suggested I spend some time with Forrest J. Gerard, his pick for assistant secretary for Indian affairs. This was an important job because it left intact the commissioner of Indian affairs, the historic job, as the operations officer for the BIA and set up the assistant secretary in a policy role.

Mark Trahant interviewing Interior Secretary Cecil Andrus in Boise, Idaho, 1979. (Courtesy photo)

Meeting Gerard changed my life. We connected almost immediately. Instead of just writing about the BIA's weaknesses, he challenged me to move to DC and try and improve things. I did just that (one of my few detours out of journalism). I learned a lot about how Washington worked in my time there (including the lesson that journalism was far more satisfying than government).

Gerard also became my life-long mentor and friend. One of the honors of my life was being able to write "The Last Great Battle of the Indian Wars" and chronicle his work on Capitol Hill. He was the author in the Senate of the Indian Self-Determination and Education Assistance Act, Indian Health Care Improvement Act, Indian Finance Act, and so many other critical pieces of legislation. He went on to serve in the Carter administration as the first Assistant Secretary of Indian Affairs.

The best newspaper in the world

There were so many great adventures at Navajo Times. We were all young — and full of a can-do spirit that defied logic. So when we asked, "Why not a daily newspaper?" We answered with action. We published every night and delivered to a geography larger than many states.

On March 21, 1984, the paper went daily. The Christian Science Monitor happened to be there: "MARK Trahant, a razor blade in one hand and a narrow strip of galley proof in the other, shoots a quick glance out the window near the sloping work table at which he stands.

'I can see the propellers going on the plane,' the youthful editor calls out to the half-dozen staffers in the cluttered newsroom housed in a ramshackle one-story building next to a dirt parking lot. It is 9:06 p.m. on Monday, March 19 — six minutes past deadline for the Navajo Times."

A daily deadline is a dance. There are steps you take during the day — and with practice it gets easier. Our delivery mechanism was an airplane loaded with newspapers. About 12:30 a.m. the plane would take off from Window Rock, fly west to Tuba City, then Black Mesa (we also served readers on the Hopi Reservation), Blanding, Utah, and finally Crownpoint, New

Mexico.

Our airplane paper route delivered newspapers even when roads were closed by snow. Our system worked.

One night I had finished editing the paper early, about 10:30 or so. I had gone to bed when I got a call: A U.S. Air Force B-52 bomber crashed near Kayenta. My first reaction was to wait for the next day, the next edition. Then I got to thinking, "No, we're a daily." So we posted a few paragraphs, a bulletin. Then Paul Natonabah, a Times photographer, and Leonard Sylvan, a printer who went along for the ride, and I headed from Window Rock to Kayenta.

Mark Trahant, editor of the Navajo Times. (Courtesy photo)

It was an adventure. And one of the key decisions I made was I told Natonabah to shoot pictures as fast as he could and then give me the film. I then rolled up the film in my jacket hood, out of view. After we were there a bit, FBI agents showed up. Their first order of business was to let us know this was a military scene and that Natonabah's camera would have to be confiscated temporarily.

But I had the film. The next day the photograph was on the front page of The Arizona Republic and in newspapers around the world via both the Associated Press and United Press International. Every image was credited to Natonabah and the Navajo Times. On that day, the Navajo Times Today was the best newspaper in the country.

The Navajo Nation's election in 1986 was a rematch between the incumbent Peterson Zah and the former chairman, Peter

MacDonald. I did something unexpected. I used to write the editorials in Navajo Times (the most talked about was only three words. When Ronald Reagan was re-elected the entire page was black, except for the words, "Four More Years.") So one day I went into my office, shut the door, and decided to endorse Zah. My logic boiled down to one reason: freedom of the press. The Navajo Times often made Zah uncomfortable — and yet he always lived up to the ideal of an independent newspaper. The only person I told was the managing editor, Monty Roessel.

The next day the staff was blown away by the editorial. Most were angry, wondering why I didn't consult them? Simple: I wanted them to be able to tell their sources they had nothing to do with it.

The MacDonald campaign created an atmosphere of inevitability. His campaign wooed the outside world, letting business and political leaders alike know that MacDonald would soon return and he would again be a force.

On election night, Nov. 4, New Mexico Sen. Pete Domenici called me in the newsroom to chat about national elections. He then asked about the tribal election. I remember him being surprised when I told him it was too close to call; he had been led to believe that a MacDonald landslide was coming. Our headline the next morning said it all: "Cliffhanger: It's MacDonald."

One of the ramifications of the election — at least for me — was that I was certain I would be fired as publisher of the Navajo Times Today. The paper was not profitable, we had endorsed his opponent and there were plenty of legitimate reasons to let me go. For weeks nothing happened — I began to think things were fine. But on Feb. 19, 1987 — a day when I was out of town — the MacDonald administration sent police to close down the newspaper. They didn't just fire me — they fired the entire staff. "Effective immediately, the

Navajo Times Today will cease publication," wrote Loyce Phoenix, MacDonald's chief executive administrator. "All employees of the Navajo Times are terminated effective today."

MacDonald's contention that the paper would lose a million dollars that year was essentially correct — especially when you include the cost of closing down the Times. What was left unsaid was an offer, including one by management, to purchase the paper. One of the tribe's lawyers told MacDonald that it was the "best opportunity" for the tribe to recover its investment.

The closing of the Navajo Times Today was expensive — especially in political terms. That very act tainted the discourse about MacDonald. Hundreds of people protested the chairman's imperial nature at the same time he closed the newspaper because of a "million-dollar loss."

And it fed a narrative about corruption — without a newspaper to keep track.

The night I was fired, the publisher of The Arizona Republic, Pat Murphy, called and offered me a job. He asked me what I would do if I had time — what story did I really want to tell? At my house in Fort Defiance, I wrote an outline for a newspaper series on federal Indian policy. The eventual series by Mike Masterson, Chuck Cook, and myself, "Fraud in Indian Country," chronicled the failures of federal policy and how the natural resource wealth of so many tribes either was mismanaged or outright stolen.

The interest in the series from Washington was incredible. Since this was pre-Internet days, every day we were faxing

INDIAN COUNTRY TODAY: THEN AND NOW

Fraud in Indian country
A billion-dollar betrayal

Indians are sold out by U.S.

Programs rife with waste, abuse, failure

By CHUCK COOK, MIKE MASTERSON and M.N. TRAHANT
The Arizona Republic

©1987, The Arizona Republic

Federal Indian programs across the United States are a shambles, plagued by fraud, incompetence and deceit and strangled by a morass of red tape that has all but destroyed their effectiveness, an investigation by *The Arizona Republic* has found.

Despite scores of billions of taxpayer dollars spent to improve Indian lives during the past century, Washington has succeeded primarily in building the most intractable and convoluted bureaucracy in the federal government.

Many Washington lawmakers and federal employees say the Bureau of Indian Affairs has earned the dubious reputation of being the worst-managed agency in the whole U.S. government.

Even the BIA's director, Ross Swimmer, during a recent interview, conceded the government's Indian programs are ineffective and plagued by abuses.

He said it is time for change.

"The best thing that could happen would be for the BIA to go away," Swimmer said. "Don't terminate the tribes, terminate the BIA ... the bureau keeps them poor."

Sen. John McCain, R-Ariz., a member of the Senate Select Committee on Indian Affairs, blasted BIA operations as inefficient and ineffective.

"The American people complain about the inefficiency and waste in the Department of Defense and are well-justified in doing so," he said.

"But if they were aware of what happens in the BIA, they would think that the Department of Defense is the one of the most efficient organizations in America, because it pales by comparison."

Federal programs for Indians have become so top-heavy even the BIA director estimates only one dollar of every 10 the government spends on Indian programs actually reaches the Indian people. The remaining 99 cents an

Indian activist Berdena Holder of Gracemont, Okla., stands by a sign put up by Indians outside the Bureau of Indian Affairs office in Anadarko, Okla. The sign protests the BIA's handling of oil royalties.

Honor system license to loot

U.S. fails to protect oil on Indian, federal lands

Oil companies have looted billions of dollars worth of oil and gas from Indian and federal lands, sometimes aided by negligent or corrupt government officials, *The Arizona Republic* has found.

A six-month investigation by the newspaper uncovered a story of government failures to carry out its responsibilities, thefts that some estimate amount to more than a billion dollars, illegal slush funds and questionably cozy relationships between oil companies and some public officials.

The federal oil and gas program, which is administered by the Bureau of Indian Affairs and two other Interior Department agencies, is so badly managed that it has shortchanged many Indians who have leased lands to oil companies, forcing onto welfare rolls some who own what should be lucrative shares in producing wells.

The program is "a system that totally relies on the good faith and trust of the (oil) producers" and whose potential for fraud is "phenomenal," according to Steven Moore, a Denver-based attorney who works with Indian issues.

Two current federal reports put recent losses at more than $11 billion, an amount equal to the tax dollars needed to run all BIA programs for more than 10 years.

But no one can put an exact dollar amount on oil and gas frauds wrought on Indian and federal lands.

A 1986 congressional study found that the federal government since 1979 has allowed oil companies to pump millions of barrels of oil from federal and Indian lands through an "honor system" that cost U.S. taxpayers and Indians an estimated $5.8 bil-

The Arizona Republic's "Fraud in Indian Country" series that exposed what the newspaper called a "billion dollar betrayal" of Native Americans, October 1987.

daily copies to folks on Capitol Hill or at the Interior Department. More than that, the Senate decided to do something. It launched a special committee to investigate the allegations raised by the newspaper. But here's the twist: the Senate's first target was MacDonald. Federal prosecutors, tribal prosecutors as well as the Senate's investigative team probed MacDonald's affairs.

This led to an internal debate on the Navajo Nation and a tragic riot in the Navajo capital (not unlike Jan. 6) and the eventual conviction of MacDonald on federal charges.

There is a story there, too. I was in The Arizona Republic when the riot started. I think I started getting calls just a few minutes after the events began to unfold. A photographer and I raced to the airport, flew to Gallup, and then took a cab to Window Rock. By then there wasn't much activity — a lot of property damage — and a group of protestors holding clubs were standing around. When we got out of the cab, someone shouted, "There's the guy who started the Senate investigation." We were surrounded and the photographer said to me, "I don't think I want to be around you right now."

But there was a great reporter moment. I reached into my back pocket and pulled out my notebook. Everyone there wanted to talk. They wanted to tell their stories about what had happened.

The long view. The thing about a 50-year reporting horizon is that I have been lucky to witness so much history. I was at The Arizona Republic writing about the legislation that followed the Cabazon decision that recognized the inherent power of tribal nations to regulate gaming. The law that followed was the Indian Gaming Regulatory Act. There are three stories worth repeating.

First: Gaming was so tiny back then; bingo was estimated to be $100 million. Hard to even fathom what's happened since, a $42 billion industry.

Second: So often the context about gaming wasn't reported by mainstream media. I grew up in a community where "Buff Vegas" saw the action of traditional games on a regular basis (for thousands of years at that). "Ah!" an editor once retorted, but one is modern, one is traditional." True enough: There are no slot machines whirring or bells clinging at Buff Vegas. But the adaptation to new technology is universal. It should never be an argument to stop tribes from doing something "modern."

Third: One of the most important pieces of misinformation came from the Indian gaming debate and that is that Congress gave tribes the right to operate casinos. The story, at first, was that Congress was limiting a Supreme Court victory, adding a regulatory framework. But a few years later it was the opposite. Most stories involving Indian gambling describe the gaming law as "giving" tribes the right to create gambling establishments on their lands. Thus, the story changed from a law that takes away a tribe's inherent right to one that "gives" tribes something.

Beyond the resume

It's impossible to capture 50 years in one essay. I don't want this to be a resume. I am grateful for every journalism home that's been a part of my life — in fact — I felt so lucky to be there. The list is long: The Salt Lake Tribune, The Seattle Times, the Moscow-Pullman Daily News, The Seattle Post-Intelligencer — and of course Indian Country Today, now ICT.

Then there are the books. I have lost count when it comes to my contribution as a chapter author of books. I am really proud of an academic journal, Daedalus, of an issue I helped edit and contributed a piece on the Indian health system.

Then there is television. My first on-air venture was for "PBS Frontline" (what a way to start). So far I have reported two stories, most recently "The Silence," about sexual abuse by priests in Alaska. Then I produced and hosted "Wassaja" for FNX: First Nations Experience. And I have done just about every job associated with the ICT newscast, including a stint as anchor and another as executive producer. I especially loved working on the climate project for ICT.

> *"If anyone in a news company ever, ever says, 'I can't find anyone' when hiring ... I will make them sit and watch all five hours. The talent from Indian Country is amazing."*
>
> – Mark Trahant

One of the highlights, of course, are election nights. Almost on a whim, ICT did an election night broadcast starting with the historic 2018 election. I wrote the next morning: "If anyone in a news company ever, ever says, 'I can't find anyone' when hiring … I will make them sit and watch all five hours. The talent from Indian Country is amazing."

And it's not just the full-time gigs. In 1988 I was covering the fires at Yellowstone National Park and just happened to have a portable short-wave radio. This was long before the internet — so you had to make an effort to get international news. An Englishman came up to me and asked: "Are you listening to the BBC?" I was and he was an editor at The Economist, and soon I was a correspondent.

The Economist was interesting because the process was so different. Instead of writing a bylined article, the work was anonymous. I would write a two- or three-page memo and the American Survey editor in London would boil that down to a few paragraphs. Lean writing long before USA Today.

Another twist on one of my dreams happened just after I joined Indian Country Today. An editor at National Geographic asked to meet. They had an issue that was soon to be published and there was a journalistic hole. "Any chance you could write something?"

Now I have always loved the idea about writing for National Geographic. Some of my friends had assignments that lasted a year or more with lots of resources for travel and a depth of reporting.

Not me. I was given a week.

I also had fun with the jobs I didn't get. I was asked to interview at MSNBC for the editor-in-chief of their digital site. That's when it was a joint venture with Microsoft and NBC. I went to NYC and hit it off the NBC folks — so much so that they asked if I could stay a couple more days (and offered to buy me clothes to make it so). But the Microsoft people and I didn't sing from the same page. It was pretty clear that a job offer wasn't happening.

The best: Stories and people

So often in my career I was where a story was unfolding. Just lucky. For example I was asked to speak in a little community in southern Ontario. And one of the other speakers that night was a legislator from Manitoba, Elijah Harper. The very night before we both spoke he had voted against the Meech Lake Accords — a constitutional process — because he said First Nations had not been a part of the negotiation.

At Kettle Point Reserve he was hailed as a conquering hero, the man who saved Canada from itself.

Another lucky moment: I ended up at a birthday party for the

Dalai Lama (at Richard Gere's house, no less). That followed by a press conference ended up as a story. Just how do you sing happy birthday? "The Big D?" "His Holiness?" No one knew.

I think I have probably interviewed hundreds of tribal leaders and heard some great stories. A few: Billy Diamond, Joe DeLaCruz, Lucy Covington, Helen Peterson, Leona Kakar, and every month when I worked in Seattle I'd have breakfast with Billy Frank Jr.

Some of the stories I will remember most are about my own family. When I was a kid, my grandmother showed me pictures of her aunt from Fort Shaw. I learned about members of the basketball team that were champions of the world. My piece: At the turn of the century, Aunt Genie had game.

When my grandmother died I wrote a column about her life in The Seattle Times. A few days later I got a call from a producer of the Oprah show. She said that it had touched people there and asked if I would consider coming on the show. (She never quite said Oprah was one, but I have to think she was.) In the end, they decided it wasn't good television. My family loved that: I was almost on Oprah.

The toughest words I have crafted were written after the death of my son, Elias. However, I also learned something from that story. I heard from a father about how Elias influenced his son and helped shape his career as a journalist, especially creating a framework for the coverage of Indigenous people. "I was blown away by that note. Where did that come from?"

This is a powerful reminder that we influence people every day in ways we do not expect.

I can't imagine how many other stories like that are still out there after 50 years of writing.

CHAPTER 2:
NOW

The Academy Awards through my eyes

By Jourdan Bennett-Begaye
ICT
March 29, 2024

This is an excerpt of the original opinion piece https://bit.ly/ICT2024academy.

LOS ANGELES — In the days following the 96th Academy Awards, I, as executive editor, the first woman and youngest to be in this role, received interesting feedback. Why was all of our coverage about the Oscars?

Naturally, I questioned, "Why not?" My second thought was this person had to be part of very few pool of Native people not watching Lily Gladstone go up against Emma Stone for leading actress.

My next thought: "This feedback has to be from a Boomer." It was. (No offense to Boomers, but we have different news consumption habits.)

The following week I received counter feedback. The reader, who was also older, said he enjoyed following our coverage of the Oscars, Lily Gladstone, and all around "Killers of the Flower Moon" as it felt similar to following Deb Haaland's journey to the secretary of the Interior Department.

This difference in opinion also means the news consumption will exist with many generations existing in Native communities. Statistics show that Native nations have a younger population than American society, so naturally we're going to be paying attention to pop culture. Pop culture and the entertainment industry, undeniably, influence the economy, politics, and many other national conversations and sectors of our world that eventually seep into our communities.

In fact this is how I became a journalist. I've watched many of the big award shows for the last 15 years or so. My Facebook friends got so tired of my award show updates that I started to create virtual watch parties. Ha. I also wanted to be the next Ryan Seacrest and interview talent on the red carpet. I loved pop culture so much as a high school and college student. From there, I saw how powerful journalism could be for Native peoples and why it's important to have more of us.

Of course, at the end of the day we always look at the numbers. According to our analytics, the top four stories were Oscars-related as of March 24. Those stories outshined our regular metrics on a monthly basis.

That meant readers wanted this material. Our editors paid

The 96th Academy Awards in Los Angeles, California, March 6, 2024. (Photo by Jourdan Bennett-Begaye, ICT)

attention and followed our instincts. We watch the trends and listen to conversations happening in Native communities.

From what we gathered, we knew it was going to be a big moment in history and needed to capture it for the record. And it was particularly important to capture history as Native journalists. That meant we had to be covering from all angles. From the Osage Nation watch party to the red carpet.

Not alone

It was exhilarating to be a Native journalist reporting at the 96th Academy Awards as this award show was a special one for Native peoples and nations. ICT Producer Paris Wise, Zia and Laguna Pueblos, captured the journey along with me.

For Hollywood's biggest night, Native peoples existed in every space imaginable. I'm saying this as a Native woman who finds myself in predominantly White spaces. So I mentally prepared myself to be the "only one"or among the very few. So when I say every space I mean from media to the press guide to ceremony attendees on the red carpet, and the drum group to Lily as Academy Award nominee.

The Academy held a b-roll session for press on Wednesday, March 6, where they'd literally roll out the red carpet for us so we could capture photos and video. Yup, this is where we get all the close-ups. I've been in journalism for a little over a decade and this was still fun to watch because, as I was taught, you have to be willing to be silly to get the good photos and videos.

Anyway, I arrived early so I could also pick up my media credentials. We could only pick them up March 5-9, and not the day of the Oscars.

I arrived at the red carpet event and as I pulled out my DSLR camera from my green purse, a press guide on the red carpet said, "I like your bag." I smiled and told them, "Thanks! It's Anishnaabe made." And they said, "Oh, I know. I lived in Anishnaabe country for some time." The individual was Chiricahua Apache and had worked for the Academy for five years and worked on this specific award show for four years. My face lit up.

Press guides were available for press folks to ask questions about anything. So naturally I asked all the questions on what to expect from shoes to snacks, to the atmosphere.

Their last piece of wisdom before I left the carpet, "Don't be shy and don't be afraid to take up space."

And I knew immediately what they meant when Oscar Sunday arrived.

Oscar prep

Our team prepped as much as we could for the Oscars. We had our Oscars Notebook ready. Assigned a few people to watch parties at Osage Nation and Montana. We planned stories to write and promote. On top of that plus reading and researching, Wise and I met up to figure out our game plan on coverage regarding where we would be and what we could capture. She was going to be in the ceremony and walking on the red carpet so she could take photos and video.

My positions were in the photo risers for the red carpet arrivals

The 96th Academy Awards red carpet in Los Angeles, California, March 6, 2024. (Photo by Jourdan Bennett-Begaye, ICT)

and in the interview room in Loew's Hollywood Hotel. The interview room is where winners go to be interviewed by journalists. The goal was to make readers feel like they were there with us.

It happened too fast.

By show time, the Red Carpet closed. I spotted Osage News Reporter Benny Polacca and we snapped photos of each other with the Oscar statue in front of the partition, and then made our way to the interview room via the press route.

The Academy provided press food as they said they wanted us to enjoy the experience. I'm glad they did because Benny, Echo and myself were so hungry.

Then off we went to our assigned spots. Echo in the photo room where winners went to take photos after they got off stage. Benny and myself in the interview room.

Hoping for a win

I sat in the Academy's interview room full of approximately 100 journalists representing 38 countries, The New York Times to my left and Osage News across from me. A poetic visual of where ICT fits in the news landscape.

Headphones in my ears, listening to the show live while we looked at the dozens of screens hanging above us. One screen in the middle showed the names and categories to help us.

After or before the photo room, winners came to our room to be interviewed. The moderator would announce the winner's name and their category. Arms holding numbers on a white paper would fly up like an auction, hoping to be one of the first to be called on to ask a question.

This room had tough rules. We couldn't take photos or videos.

INDIAN COUNTRY TODAY: THEN AND NOW

The Academy provided a transcript to us via the Academy Portal online, which we had to register for ahead of time. Press could also ask questions virtually. If we had calls to talk, take them outside.

Fingers flew away at the keyboards while winners talked on stage. People whispered or continued to listen to the show during interviews. Everyone in tuxedos or floor-length gowns.

One by one we went through the program given to us, which also could change at any moment, but it was a guide.

Then the leading actress came up next. "And the Oscar goes to…" read last year's Oscar winner for Best Actress Michelle Yeoh. She closes the envelope with a smile. "Emma Stone." Loud gasps echoed in the interview room. Next to me the older, White male journalist said, "WHAT?!"

Lily Gladstone at the 96th Academy Awards in Los Angeles, March 6, 2024. (Photo by Jourdan Bennett-Begaye, ICT)

The air left my chest. I didn't know what to say.

A few minutes later I looked at Benny and did the hashtag sign with my hands saying, "Oscars Still So White."

The Black reporter next to him in a beautiful gown said, "The fact that everyone in this room was surprised."

I immediately messaged our reporting and editing team, and then my sister. Collective sadness, disappointment, and shock.

I didn't ask how Benny felt but I was extremely bummed that we weren't going to be the first to ask Lily Gladstone, the first

Native American woman to be nominated for Best Actress, questions of her win, of her journey, and so much more. The Academy gave priority to Osage News and ICT to be the first newsrooms to ask Lily questions if she won.

Emotions flooded social media.

I learned so much from this experience. To be brave. To take up space. To have fun. But also the lesson of "two things can be true at once" sunk in. We can be happy Lily made it this far in the game because she took us this far AND we can also be disappointed by the results. This world isn't black and white. It's extremely gray.

As I packed up and took the laminated card stock paper with our name on it, the experience began to hit me. It still does to this day. I just covered the 96th Academy Awards in-person. It was everything and more that I expected it to be.

Osage dancers at the 96th Academy Awards in Los Angeles, California, March 6, 2024. (Photo by Jourdan Bennett-Begaye, ICT)

Historic Apology: Boarding school history 'a sin on our soul'

By Mary Annette Pember, Shondin Mayo and Mark Trahant
ICT
October 25, 2024

WARNING: This story contains disturbing details about residential and boarding schools. If you are feeling triggered, here is a <u>resource list for trauma responses</u> from the National Native American Boarding School Healing Coalition in the U.S. In Canada, the National Indian Residential School Crisis Hotline can be reached at 1-866-925-4419.

GILA RIVER INDIAN COMMUNITY — President Joe Biden delivered a historic apology Friday on behalf of the United States for the nation's dark past with Indian boarding schools, which sought to wipe out Native people, culture and language.

Calling the federal boarding school policies "a sin on our soul," Biden drew cheers, tears and at least one protester among the hundreds of the mostly Indigenous crowd gathered for the long-awaited announcement.

"After 150 years, the government eventually stopped the program (of boarding schools) but never formally apologized," Biden told the crowd. "I formally apologize today as President of the United States of America for what we did. I apologize, apologize, apologize!

"This apology is long overdue and quite frankly there is no excuse this apology took 50 years to make," he said. "The pain that this has caused will always be a significant mark of shame."

Biden, in his first visit to tribal lands as president, was introduced to the crowd by Gila River Gov. Stephen Roe Lewis.

"Each of us understands the solemn nature of this day, this moment, this historical time and place that we are all a part of," Lewis said, praising the Biden administration's work with tribal communities. "Today's words will be carried forward by all of us here. This is a day built on respect and honor."

Biden outlined his administration's work with tribal communities over the last four years with infrastructure, water, language revitalization, tribal development and recognition of tribal sovereignty.

But he didn't address specifics about the work that lies ahead for the government to help tribal communities heal from the generational trauma that endures from the boarding school

President Biden at the Gila Crossing Community School in Laveen, Arizona, October 25, 2024. (Photo by Shondiin Mayo, ICT)

era.

U.S. Interior Secretary Deb Haaland, Laguna Pueblo, in her speech handing off to Biden, referenced a "10-year national plan driven by tribal leaders" that will include efforts to revitalize Native languages that many students were beaten for speaking.

Haaland, the first Native American to serve in a presidential cabinet, introduced herself in her Native language.

"Today is a day for remembering, but it's also a day to celebrate our perseverance," Haaland said, at one point choking up in tears. "In spite of everything that has happened, we are still here. We are here, healing our souls .... And we are still here doing our best to speak our languages, even if our parents were afraid to teach us. Thank you, Mr. President, for bringing us together."

Reactions from survivors

The apology drew broad support from survivors, families, congressional leaders, tribal officials, elders and younger generations of Native people. But many emphasized that the apology is just a first step in helping families and tribal communities heal from the generational traumas of boarding schools.

"I think the spirits of those children who went to (boarding)

U.S. Interior Secretary Deb Haaland at the Gila Crossing Community School in Laveen, Arizona, October 25, 2024. (Photo by Shondiin Mayo, ICT)

school before me rejoiced," said Matthew War Bonnet, 78, Sicangu Lakota from the Rosebud reservation in South Dakota, who attended the announcement Friday. War Bonnet attended St. Francis Mission School for eight years, beginning at age 6. "It needs to go further and I think it will be an ongoing process, just as it was for us to acknowledge all that happened at the school," he said.

James LaBelle, Iñupiaq, who survived the Wrangell Institute and Edgecumbe High School, was also in the audience Friday at Gila River. "Biden's apology was very heartfelt,' said LaBelle, a past president of the National Native American Boarding School Healing Coalition. "He mentioned all of the harms included in the boarding school era, acknowledged all the abuses we experienced; he didn't leave anything out. "I feel emotional and overwhelmed," he said, "but also know that now the real work begins."

Mark Macarro, chairman of the Pechanga Band of Luiseño Indians in California and president of the National Congress of American Indians who also attended the announcement, said the apology is "a necessary step" and "foundational."

"I don't think it's possible to move forward into any type of healing, any type of reconciliation until you have the apology," Macarro said. "People often these days seem to discount the value of the formal announcement of an apology, an actual apology being done … But it really can't be overstated how important this step is. It is rare for a president, a world leader, to apologize for the actions of a country, a country's citizens, against another group of citizens within that country."

But more is needed, he said. "I think it's really never going to be enough," he said. "But that's one of the areas where that certainly needs focus because that was one of the direct impacts, or destructive impacts, of the boarding schools."

INDIAN COUNTRY TODAY: THEN AND NOW

A long process

The apology Friday, Oct. 25, came after an introduction that included traditional singers and dancers from Gila River, Salt River dressed in tribal regalia, the men rhythmically playing shakers as women sang.

The performances provided an air of ceremony and respectful celebration on three separate stages with backdrops emblazoned with the Gila River language announcing the owners of the lands on which they stood.

Elders, many of them boarding school survivors, sat in the shade, shielding their eyes from the sun, waiting for words that had been too long in coming.

It also came after years of work in the Department of the Interior, which includes the Bureau of Indian Affairs, and a year-long effort by Haaland and Assistant Secretary for Indian Affairs Bryan Newland, who traveled across the country gathering testimony from boarding school survivors and families as part of a "Road to Healing Tour."

A final investigative report on Indian boarding schools released in July by the Department of the Interior called for a formal apology from the U.S., but also issued other recommendations, including Congressional approval of a proposed Truth and Healing Commission to further investigate boarding schools, a national memorial to acknowledge those who endured the hardships, and financial support for tribal programs that include repatriation, education, mental health support and community rebuilding.

A bill that would create the Truth and Healing Commission, with authority to subpoena records from church-run boarding schools, is pending in Congress. Officials have been hoping to get it passed by the end of the year, but the likelihood of that appears uncertain.

Tens of thousands of Native children were coerced or forcibly removed from their families to attend boarding schools, starting in the 1800s and continuing into the 20th century. The schools operated under a policy of forced assimilation that kept them isolated from their families, culture and language.

Biden did not mince words in describing the horrors endured by children at the schools, where staff took their traditional clothes, cut their hair and often abused them, psychologically, physically or sexually.

Biden noted in addition to the abuse, some children were put up for adoption, and others died at schools and were buried, some in unmarked graves.

"Trauma and shame passed down through generations," he said.

He said the apology "to me is one of the most consequential things I've ever had to do."

He asked the crowd for a moment of silence to remember those lost and the generations who have lived with the trauma.

"For our nation, it was too shameful to acknowledge," he said, adding, "While darkness can hide much, it erases nothing … We do not erase history, we make history, we learn history, and we remember, so we can heal as a nation."

Also contributing to this report were ICT staff members Kevin Abourezk, Nika Bartoo-Smith, Kalle Benalle, Felix Clary, Pauly Denetclaw, Stewart Huntington, Kolby KickingWoman, Kadin Mills, Miles Morrisseau, Luna Reyna, Amelia Schafer, Shirley Sneve, Mark Trahant and Quindrea Yazzie.

CHAPTER 3:
ICT AND INDIJ PUBLIC MEDIA

A new day, a new ICT

By Jourdan Bennett-Begaye
ICT
June 23, 2022

More than two years ago, George Floyd's murder sparked national conversations about police reform, racial injustice, and our own biases.

Our newsroom saw that our name, "Indian Country Today," though a strong brand and recognizable name anywhere, was also outdated. Our style guide had this entry for ICT:

> *"Many readers have said that the term "Indian" represents the past and have asked why we don't change our name?"*
>
> – Aliyah Chazev

"Many readers have said that the term 'Indian' represents the past and have asked us why we don't change our name? Fact is, if we were starting from scratch we would likely go another route. But brands are powerful and Indian Country Today is a case in point: Readers know where to find us; something that would be lost with a name change. We should always be mindful, however, about the terms history and especially our use of symbols associated with the word. It's unacceptable to become the very mascot we object to in professional sports or media."

That style entry is four years old, from when we started from scratch again in 2018 using the name. That brand attracted 6.6 million people every year to our digital platform and now a national television broadcast in 37 states with an international audience. The broadcast will reach all 50 states starting in July. We were right four years ago; brands are powerful. What's even more powerful is the talent in the newsroom and voices in our communities. Over the course of a year, Candis Callison, Tałtan and journalism professor at the University of British Columbia, facilitated conversations in our newsrooms about a possible name change. Those conversations were very insightful due to the makeup of our newsroom, from interns to veteran journalists, and the ranges of backgrounds and experiences.

Everyone had their ears to the ground, bringing community voices with them. This country and Indigenous nations and peoples are moving in a new direction of inclusiveness and equity. That means we had to consider the term "Indian" in our name. "Indian" is often a term used by the elder generation because that's what the government called them and they called themselves. It's in federal documents. If you ever hear elders speak and say "Indians," they say it without flinching.

ICT's mission is to build the next generation of storytellers and to build a sustainable news organization for them. Times are changing. Innovation and evolution are needed. The facilitated conversations with Callison led to renaming "Indian

Country Today" to ICT.

ICT captures all the generations and voices in our communities and newsroom. It can still mean Indian Country Today to those who know its legacy and brand. It can also take on the name of Indigenous Communities
Today, Indigenous Cultures Today, or more. We are leaving it up to interpretation of our readers. Along with the name is a new logo. The late Shon Quannie, Acoma Pueblo, designed the turtle logo for ICT. That logo is now used for ICT's parent company, IndiJ Public Media. We wanted to keep on his legacy and worked with Jill Neumeister of Orca Design Group, who admired Quannie's work from afar. The new logo signifies a ribbon skirt. To show the matriarchal power in Indigenous communities.

Our organization is made up of majority Native women as well as the leadership. The colors on the logo represent the different owners of ICT throughout its 40 years. Blue for its founding by Tim Giago and initially known as The Lakota Times. Purple for the Oneida Nation of New York. Orange represents the National Congress of American Indians. Red for ICT now, the constant thread and foundation of who we are: Indigenous news by Indigenous journalists for Indigenous peoples.

What's IndiJ Public Media?

By Janee' Doxtator
IndiJ Public Media and ICT
Marketing and Communications Director

IndiJ Public Media, the nonprofit parent company of ICT, is reintroducing itself while reminding you that ICT (formerly Indian Country Today) has been sharing newsworthy stories from trusted journalists since 1981. ICT has evolved from The Lakota Times newspaper to a national magazine, a digital publication, and now a multimedia organization with a half-hour newscast.

The rebrand of IndiJ Public Media began last fall, marked by our new website URL, indijpublicmedia.org. As CEO Karen Michel, Ho-Chunk, stated, "Our focus remains on Indigenous journalism while emphasizing our expansion into broadcasting."

Established in 2021, IndiJ Public Media partnered with ObsidianWeb to redesign the website, transforming it into a hub for all things related to IndiJ Public Media. ObsidianWeb President and CEO Rocky Tano expressed his pride in contributing to our mission, highlighting the organization's support for Native-owned businesses.

As part of this transformation, the IndiJ Public Media logo was refreshed to honor the legacy of the late Shon Quannie, who designed the original Indian Country Today logo. The change was necessary as ICT transitioned into broadcasting, choosing a name that reflects the diverse ways Indigenous people shape language today. "As a colleague and close friend of the late Shon Quannie, undertaking this project was a way for me to pay respects and honor the legacy he left behind," said Tano.

Aliyah Chavez, host of ICT Newscast, explained the name change during ICT's 40th-anniversary livestream. "Our audience has reminded us that the term 'Indian Country' was given by non-Native people; it's language used in broken treaties and policies imposed on our ancestors. Our new name reflects how Indigenous people want to be called, aiming to be more inclusive of the many ways Indigenous people are shaping the language of the future."

The ICT logo was inspired by traditional ribbon skirts and the stories they tell. The colors represent key milestones in our history: blue for our roots in The Lakota Times, purple for the Oneida Nation's acquisition in 1998, orange for our transition to the National Congress of American Indians in 2017, and red for the name change to ICT in 2021. "This is a new day for ICT, which has a long history as a premier source of news for and about Indigenous communities, written and produced by Indigenous journalists," said Michel.

The ICT brand includes the award-winning digital news site ICTNews.org and "ICT Newscast with Aliyah Chavez," covering the Indigenous world, including American Indians and Alaska Natives. ICT's broadcast is carried via public television stations, including FNX: First Nations Experience, Arizona PBS World, and the World channel, and is delivered directly to our email subscribers.

You may have already encountered the IndiJ Public Media brand through our "New Look, Deeper Impact" initiative or when making a donation to support the free Indigenous news we provide to communities. Our branding video, to be released on Monday, August 26, [2024,] explains who IndiJ Public Media is in relation to ICT and how ICT evolved from Tim Giago's Lakota Times and Indian Country Today.

We invite you to be a part of this mission. Visit <u>ICT</u> and <u>IndiJ Public Media</u> — and become a member today.

INDIAN COUNTRY TODAY: THEN AND NOW

OUR BRAND EVOLUTION

1981 — THE LAKOTA TIMES - ICT was launched as The Lakota Times, a for-profit newspaper by the late journalist Tim Giago of the Oglala Lakota Nation in South Dakota.

1992 — NATIONAL EXPANSION - The Lakota Times changed its name to Indian Country Today to reflect its national focus and broader reach.

1998 — A NEW HOME - Indian Country Today was sold to Standing Stone Media, Inc., an operation of the Oneida Nation of New York, which continued to operate the publication as a news magazine.

2011 — THE DIGITAL AGE - Indian Country Today entered the digital scene and transitioned to an online operation as Indian Country Today Media Network.

2017 — END OF AN ERA - After 35 years of award-winning reporting, Indian Country Today was donated to the National Congress of American Indians and went dark.

2018 — REBIRTH - To fill the gap in Indigenous journalism, Indian Country Today was revived by the National Congress of American Indians as a digital startup under the leadership of Mark Trahant.

2020 — A NEW MODEL - IndiJ Public Media was established as an Arizona 501(c)(3) nonprofit to create a new model based on Indigenous values and to empower Indian Country Today.

2021 — A VISION FORWARD - Ownership was transferred to IndiJ Public Media, and Indian Country Today evolved into ICT, a multimedia news organization.

2024 — THE FUTURE - IndiJ Public Media continues transforming the nonprofit newsrooms by further expansion in Indigenous regions via partnerships to bring relevant local reporting.

OUR STAFF

OUR INDIJ PUBLIC MEDIA STAFF

President and CEO   Karen Michel | Ho-Chunk

Chief Finance and Administrative Officer   Laura Fuentes

Chief Information Officer   Sky Vasquez | Bishop Paiute

Chief of Staff   Jacki Foster | Chickasaw Nation

Senior Director of Revenue   Heather Donovan

Donor Relations Director   Haley Martinez

Marketing and Communications Director   Janee' Doxtator | Oneida Nation

Marketing and Social Media Manager   Alexandra Keenan

Grants Manager   Emily Matis

Account Executive   Courtney Habrock

Development Specialist   Steven Mowatt | Comanche Nation of Oklahoma

Administrative Assistant and Accounting Coordinator   Sydnie Turner

OUR ICT NEWS STAFF

General Manager   Ebonye Delaney

News Director   Dianna Hunt | Cherokee Nation

Managing Editor   Jourdan Bennett-Begaye | Diné

Deputy Managing Editor   Kevin Abourezk | Rosebud Sioux

Mountain Bureau Chief   Kolby KickingWoman | Blackfeet/Gros Ventre

Northwest Bureau Chief   **Luna Reyna | Montana Little Shell Chippewa

Senior Multimedia Producer   Shirley Sneve | Ponca/Sicangu Lakota

Multimedia Producer   Paris Wise | Zia/Laguna Pueblo

Multimedia Producer   Stewart Huntington

National Correspondent   Mary Annette Pember | Red Cliff Band of Ojibwe

Multimedia Journalist   Daniel Herrera Carbajal

Multimedia Journalist   *Erica Ayis

Multimedia Journalist   Kalle Benallie | Navajo Nation

Multimedia Journalist   **Nika Bartoo-Smith | Osage/Oneida Nation

Multimedia Journalist   Pauly Denetclaw | Diné

Shared journalist with PBS Wisconsin   **Shared journalist with Underscore Native News

ABOUT THE CONTRIBUTORS

Jourdan Bennett-Begaye, Diné, is the managing editor of IndiJ Public Media/ICT. Based in the Nacotchtank and Piscataway Lands of Washington, DC, Bennett-Begaye received her master's degree in magazine, newspaper, and online journalism at Syracuse University and a bachelor's degree in athletic training from Fort Lewis College (FLC). She serves as the Vice President on the board of directors for the Indigenous Journalism Association and dedicates her time to many causes. Bennett-Begaye has won multiple awards including the 2022 Richard LaCourse Award, an investigative journalism award, and received FLC's Alumni Rising Star award in 2023.

Janee' Doxtator, Oneida Nation, is the marketing and communications director of IndiJ Public Media/ICT. Based in Virginia, Doxtator manages the organization's brand strategy, audience development, and marketing efforts. She has an MBA from Capella University, a master's degree from Cardinal Stritch University, and a bachelor's degree in Journalism and Mass Communications from the University of Wisconsin-Milwaukee. Doxtator has served as a liaison for Indigenous communities and has lent her knowledge of marketing, public relations, and cultural communications as a board and committee member and published author. She was appointed to the Governor's Council on Tourism and the recipient of two Excellence in Action Awards.

Karen Lincoln Michel, Ho-Chunk, is president, CEO and chief editorial officer of IndiJ Public Media/ICT. Based in Wisconsin, Michel leads the business and editorial operations. She has a bachelor's degree in industrial technology from the University of Wisconsin-Stout, a master's degree in journalism from Marquette University, and has an honorary doctorate degree in humane letters from Marquette. She is a past president of the Native American

Journalists Association, past president of UNITY: Journalists of Color, a former member of the Friends Board of PBS Wisconsin, and serves on the IndiJ Public Media Board of Directors.

Mark Trahant, Shoshone-Bannock Tribes, is a freelance journalist and the former editor of IndiJ Public Media/ICT. Based in Arizona, Trahant has been a reporter, television correspondent, speaker, teacher, and author who has worked to provide opportunities for those whose voices are not often heard. He has received many honors including being recognized by The National Native American Hall of Fame and was nominated for a Pulitzer Prize for National Reporting in 1988. Trahant has held numerous chair positions and on served many boards, committees, and task forces. He has worked as a journalist for more than fifty years and continues to have a lasting impact.

Mary Annette Pember, Red Cliff Band of Lake Superior Chippewa, is a national correspondent of IndiJ Public Media/ICT. Based in Ohio, Pember reports on news from coast to coast and has covered pertinent Native American issues. She is the recipient of several media industry awards and fellowships including The Clarion Award, several Associated Press awards, the Medill Lifetime Achievement Award as well as fellowships with Type Investigations Ida B. Wells, Rosalynn Carter Mental Health Journalism, and the University of S. California Annenberg National Health Fellowship. Pember's work has appeared in several media venues and is a published book author.

Shondiin Mayo, Diné and Koyukon Athabascan, is an IJA-ASU-ICT Fellow. Based in Alaska, Mayo is a freelance multimedia journalist who has learned values such as an appreciation for the land, the preservation of traditional knowledge, and the responsibility to continue her heritage. She graduated from Northern Arizona University (NAU) with a bachelor's degree in Creative Media and Film, with a focus on Documentary, and is pursuing a graduate degree in Mass Communication at Arizona State University. Mayo continues spotlighting marginalized voices in her local news reporting and is dedicated to bridging gaps between Indigenous communities and mainstream media.

INDIAN COUNTRY TODAY: THEN AND NOW

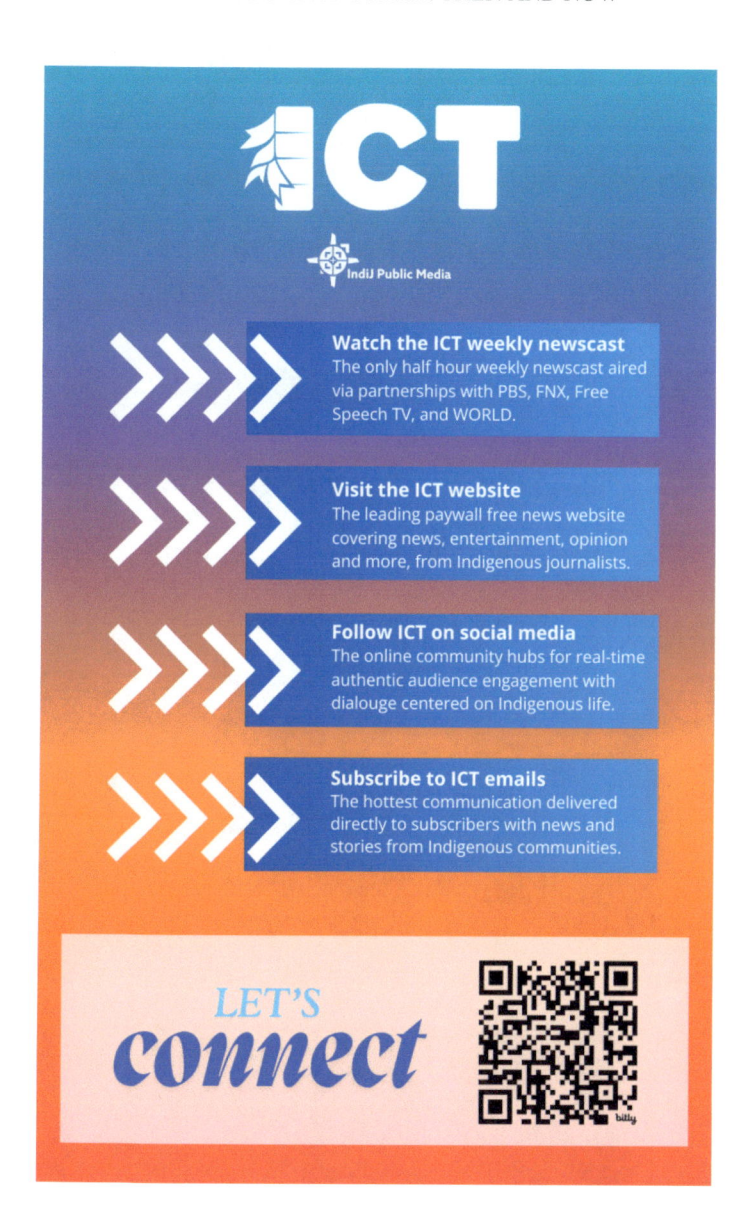

ICT
IndiJ Public Media

Watch the ICT weekly newscast
The only half hour weekly newscast aired via partnerships with PBS, FNX, Free Speech TV, and WORLD.

Visit the ICT website
The leading paywall free news website covering news, entertainment, opinion and more, from Indigenous journalists.

Follow ICT on social media
The online community hubs for real-time authentic audience engagement with dialouge centered on Indigenous life.

Subscribe to ICT emails
The hottest communication delivered directly to subscribers with news and stories from Indigenous communities.

LET'S *connect*

Made in the USA
Columbia, SC
02 July 2025